A NORTHERN CHRISTMAS

A NORTHERN CHRISTMAS

BY

ROCKWELL KENT

With a Foreword by Doug Capra

WESLEYAN UNIVERSITY PRESS

Published by University Press of New England

Hanover and London

Wesleyan University Press
Published by University Press of New England,
Hanover, NH 03755
© 1998 by Wesleyan University Press
Foreword © 1998 by Doug Capra
Reprinted by arrangement with the Rockwell Kent Legacies from
the 1941 edition published by American Artists Group, Inc.
Printed in Singapore
5 4 3 2 1

Library of Congress Cataloging-in-Publication Data
Kent, Rockwell, 1882–1971.
A northern Christmas / Rockwell Kent ; foreword by Doug Capra.
p.   cm.
Originally published: New York : American Artists Group, 1941.
ISBN 0–8195–6362–5 (cl. : alk. paper)
1. Kent, Rockwell, 1882–1971.
2. Artists—United States—Biography.
3. Renard Island (Alaska)—Description and travel.
4. Christmas—Alaska—Renard Island.   I. Title.
N6537.K44A2   1998
760'.092—dc21
[B]   98–8211

FOREWORD

WHENEVER I reread *A Northern Christmas* by Rockwell Kent, I am struck by a sentence from his Christmas Eve 1918 journal entry: "I suppose the greatest festivals of our lives are those at which we dance ourselves."

At age thirty-six, the New York artist found himself with his nine-year-old son on Fox Island at the entrance to Resurrection Bay, about twelve miles south of Seward, Alaska. This was no romantic retreat for an artist in search of peace and beauty but rather "the flight to freedom of a man who detests the endless petty quarrels and the bitterness of the crowded world—the pilgrimage of a philosopher in quest of happiness and peace of mind." It was to be no easy quest.

Lars Olson, a seventy-one-year-old Swede and Alaskan pioneer who ran a goat and fox farm on the island, welcomed the Kents by offering them an old goat shed. Kent took up the challenge and created a comfortable refuge. Disgusted with a money-hungry world at war, struggling to save his marriage, and desperate to earn a living with his art, Kent teetered on the brink of what he called the "emptiness of the abyss" before eventually filling that void with the wealth of his own soul.

As Christmas approaches on Fox Island, Kent choreographs his own dance, teaches the steps to his son and Olson, and even provides the music with his flute. "You need nothing from outside," he writes, "not even illusion." The artist, his son, and the old man brighten the winter darkness with a candle-lit tree, hang spruce and hemlock boughs for decoration, make do with homemade and improvised gifts, and cook up a Christmas feast announced with hand-printed menus. He has again fulfilled a life-long goal by creating his culture rather than being created by it.

Back in New York after seven months in Alaska, and encouraged by a successful show of his sketches, Kent wrote *Wilderness: A Journal of Quiet Adventure in Alaska*. Its publication in 1920, timed to coincide with a show of his Alaska paintings, began Kent's rise to fame. Years later, he excerpted the Christmas chapters from *Wilderness*, made some minor changes to them, and designed a gift book published in 1941 by the American Artists Group. With this fine reproduction of the first edition, we are fortunate to have *A Northern Christmas* back in print.

Seward, Alaska   Doug Capra
March 1998

A NORTHERN CHRISTMAS

A NORTHERN CHRISTMAS

BEING THE STORY OF A PEACEFUL
CHRISTMAS IN THE REMOTE AND
PEACEFUL WILDERNESS OF AN
ALASKAN ISLAND

BY

ROCKWELL KENT

NEW YORK • AMERICAN ARTISTS GROUP

To

EVERYBODY

A MERRY CHRISTMAS AND

A HAPPY NEW YEAR

THE south coast of the mainland of Alaska is a wilderness of spruce-clad mountains whose outlying, isolated peaks are islands. On one of these we lived, a father and his eight-year son. We lived there in the winter of nineteen-eighteen and nineteen, the man in pursuit of his profession, the boy in pursuit of what of education lay in doing things, and both in that pursuit of happiness which, with whatever right, is still what every living creature wants. They had come a long long way, these two: and what they sought they found. If home is where what you desire is, then we'd come home.

There in the forest on a low-lying level fill between two mountain peaks we lived: our house a one room cabin crudely built of logs and caulked with moss; our dooryard—

toward the view—the space we'd cleared by
felling trees for fuel; our view a crescent
cove, the bay, the mountains of the distant
shore, the sky, the moon and stars at night.
And, for companionship, ourselves, each
other, and a genial, wise and kind old man,
old Sourdough of early gold rush days, old
trapper, lifelong pioneer, a Swede named
Olson: we three, a pair of foxes shut in a
corral, a milk goat (christened Nanny), an
obstreperous Angora goat (one Billy) and
some foolishly adoring women of his kind,
otters that now and then sat basking on the
rocks, blue jays and gulls, and porcupines.
It was enough. Of the fullness of the days
—fullness of work and thought, of play, of
little happenings, of uneventful peace—we

kept record.

That record is a book: its name is *WILD-ERNESS*. From *WILDERNESS* these notes about a happy Christmas in the north are drawn.

Thursday, December nineteenth

This day is never to be forgotten, so beautiful, so calm, so still with the earth and every branch and tree muffled in deep, feathery, new-fallen snow. And all day the softest clouds have drifted lazily over the heaven, shrouding the land here and there in veils of falling snow, while elsewhere or through the snow itself the sun shone. Golden shadows, dazzling peaks, fairy tracery of branches against the blue summer sea! It was a day to Live,—and work could be forgotten.

So Rockwell and I explored the woods, at first reverently treading one path, so that the snow about us might still lie undisturbed. But soon the cub in the boy broke out and he rolled in the deepest thickets, shook the trees down upon himself, lay still in the snow for me to cover him completely, washed his face till it was crimson, and wound up with a naked snow-bath. I photographed him standing thus in the deep snow at the water's edge with the mountains far off behind him. Then he dried himself at the roaring fire we'd made ready and felt like a new boy— if that can be imagined. Meanwhile I searched in the woods for a Christmas tree and cut a fair-sized one at last for its top. Christmas is right upon us now. To-night the cranberries stew on the stove.

Friday, December twentieth

The beautiful snow is fast going under the falling rain! With only five more days before Christmas it is probable we'll have little if any snow on the ground then. A snowless Christmas in Alaska!

This day was as uneventful as could be. Part of the morning was consumed in putting a new handle into the sledge hammer. It was

too dark to paint long, hardly an hour of daylight. These days slip by so easily and with so little accomplished! Only by burning midnight oil can much be done.

Sunday, December twenty-second

Both yesterday and to-day it has poured rain. They've not been unpleasant days, however. Occasional let-ups have allowed us to cut wood and get water without inconvenience.

Both days I have been occupied with humble, house-wifely duties,—baking, washing, mending, and now the cabin is adorned

with our drying clothes. Here, where water must be carried so far, it is the wet days that are wash days. Darning is a wretched nuisance. We should have socks enough to tide us over our stay here. Last night after Rockwell had been put to bed I sat down and did two of the best drawings I have made. At half past twelve I finished them, and then to calm my elation a bit for sleep read in the "Odyssey."

Ten days from now it comes due for Olson to go to Seward. If only then we have mild, calm weather! But as yet we have seen no steamer go to Seward since early in the month. It looks as if the steamship companies had combined to deprive Alaska of its Christmas mail and freight in a policy of making the deadlock with the government over the mail contracts intolerable. Meanwhile, instead of serving us, the jaunty little

naval cruisers that summered here in idleness
doubtless loaf away the winter months in
comfortable southern ports.

Monday, December twenty-third

Up to this morning the hard warm rain
continued, and now the stars are all out and
it might be thought a night in spring. At
eight-thirty I walked over in sneakers and
underwear for a moment's call on Olson, but
he had gone to bed. And now, although
we'll have no snow, the weather is fair for
Christmas.

If Olson believes, as he says, that Christmas will pass as any other day, he is quite
wrong. The tree waits to be set up and it
will surely be a thing of beauty, blazing with
its many candles in this somber log interior.
I've given up the idea of dressing Olson as

Santa Claus in goat's wool whiskers. Santa Claus without presents would move us to tears. There are a few little gifts,—a pocket-knife and a kitchen set of knife, fork, and a can-opener for Olson. An old broken fountain pen for Rockwell, some sticks of candy, —and the dinner! What shall it be? Wait!

It is midnight. I've just finished a good drawing. The lamp is about at its accustomed low mark—yesterday it had to be filled twice! Those nights when without a clock I sat up so late and to so uncertain an hour I have discovered by the lamp and the clock to-gether to have been really long. My bed-time then was after two or three o'clock— but I arose later. To-day I finished a little picture for Olson, and so did Rockwell. These were forgotten in my list of presents as I've just written it. I have shown in my picture the king of the island himself striding out to feed the goats while Billy, rearing on his hind legs, tries to steal the food on the way. Rockwell's picture is of Olson surrounded by all the goats in a more peaceful mood. Olson's cabin is in the background. I wish we had more to give the good old man. At any rate he dines with us.

Christmas Eve!

We've cleaned the house, stowed everything away upon shelves and hooks and in
corners, moved even my easel aside; dec-
orated the roof timbers with dense hemlock
boughs, stowed quantities of wood behind
the stove—for there must be no work on that
holiday—and now both Rockwell and I are
in a state of suppressed excitement over to-
morrow.

What a strange thing! Nothing is coming
to us, no change in any respect in the routine

of our lives but what we make ourselves,—and yet the day looms so large and magnificent before us! I suppose the greatest festivals of our lives are those at which we dance ourselves. You need nothing from outside,—not even illusion. Certainly children need to be given scarcely an idea to develop out of it an atmosphere of mystery and expectation as real and thrilling to themselves as if it rested upon true belief.

Well, the tree is ready, cut to length with a cross at the foot to stand upon, and a cardboard and tin-foil star to hang at its top. And now as to Christmas weather. This morning, as might just as well have been expected, was again overcast. Toward evening light snow began to fall. It soon turned to rain and the rain now has settled down to a gentle, even, all-night-and-day pace. Let it snow or rain and grow dark at midday! The better shall be our good Christmas cheer within. This is the true Christmas land. The day should be dark, the house further overshadowed by the woods, tall and black. And there in the midst of that somber, dreadful gloom the Christmas tree should blaze in glory unrivaled by moon or sun or star.

Christmas Day on Fox Island

It is mild; the ground is almost bare and a warm rain falls. First, the Christmas tree all dripping wet is brought into the house and set upon its feet. It is nine feet and a half high and just touches the peak of the cabin. There it stands and dries its leaves while Rockwell and I prepare the feast.

Both stoves are kept burning and the open door lets in the cool air. Everything goes beautifully; the wood burns as it should, the oven heats, the kettle boils, the beans stew, the bread browns in the oven just right, and the new pudding sauce foams up as rich and delicious as though instead of the first it were

the hundredth time I'd made it. And now
everything is ready. The clock stands at a
quarter to three. Night has about fallen and
lamp light is in the cabin.

"Run, Rockwell, out-of-doors and play
awhile." Quickly I stow the presents about
the tree, hang sticks of candy from it, and
light the candles.

Rockwell runs for Mr. Olson, and just as
they approach the cabin the door opens and

fairyland is revealed to them. It is wonderful. The interior of the cabin is illuminated
as never before, as perhaps no cabin interior
ever was among these wild mountains. Then
all amazed and wondering those two children
come in. Who knows which is the more en-
tranced?

Then Olson and I drink in deep solemnity
a silent toast; and the old man says, "I'd
give everything—yes, everything I have in
the world to have your wife here now!"

FOX ISLAND, CHRISTMAS
1918

Olives   Pickles

Spaghetti a la Fox Island

Beans a la Resurrection Bay

Murphies en Casserole

Cranberry Sauce

Plum Pudding Magnifique

Sauce a la Alaska Rum

Demi Tasse

Nuts   Raisins   Bon-bons

Home Sweet Home Cider

—

Music by the German Band

And the presents are handed out. For
Olson this picture from Rockwell. Ah, he
thinks it's wonderful! Then for Rockwell this
book—a surprise from Seward. Next for
Olson a painting, a kitchen set, and a pocket-

knife. By this time he's quite overcome. It's the first Christmas he has ever had! And Rockwell, when he is handed two old copies of the "Geographic Magazine," cries in amazement, "Why I thought I was to have no presents!" But in addition he gets a pocket-knife and the broken fountain pen and sits on the bed looking at the things as though they were the most wonderful of gifts.

Dinner is now set upon the table. Olson adjusts his glasses and reads the formal menu that lies at his place.

So we feast and have a jolly good time. It is a true party and looks like one.

Rockwell and I are in clean white shirts, Olson is magnificent in a new flannel shirt and his Sunday trousers and waistcoat. He wears a silk tie with a gold nugget pin. He is shaven, and clipped about the ears. How grand he looks! The food is good and plentiful, the night is long, only the Christmas candles are short-lived and we extinguish them to save them for another time. Finally, as the night deepens, Olson leaves us amid mutual expressions of delight in one another's friendship, and Rockwell and I tumble into bed.

So ended Christmas on Fox Island. As life had been, so, after Christmas, it went on. With spring, too soon, the time for our enforced departure came. We left Fox Island. Tearfully, on the threshold of the world, I wrote, concluding *WILDERNESS:*

And now at last it is over. Fox Island will soon become in our memories like a dream or vision, a remote experience too wonderful for the full liberty we knew there and the deep peace to be remembered or believed in as a real experience in life. It was for us life as it should be, serene and wholesome; love—but no hate, faith without disillusionment, the absolute for the toiling hands of man and for his soaring spirit. Olson of the deep experience, strong, brave, generous and gentle like a child; and his island—like Paradise. Ah God,—and now the world again!

This is Book Number One in the series of the American Artists Group Gift Books. The type used for the text is twelve-point Cloister bold. The illustrations and the book jacket are by Rockwell Kent. Most of the text and pictures are from WILDERNESS, A Journal of Quiet Adventure in Alaska, published by G. P. Putnam's Sons, New York. Grateful acknowledgement is made of the publisher's courtesy.

ROCKWELL KENT (1882–1971) was one of America's most celebrated graphic artists. At the height of his career, during the 1930s and 1940s, his artwork appeared virtually everywhere. Although his illustrations for Shakespeare's *Complete Works* and *Moby Dick* may be his most famous artistic achievements, Kent also created the "random house" that, despite revision through the years, has been the colophon of that company since its inception in 1928. A highly vocal political activist, Kent's refusal to comply with McCarthy's Committee on Un-American Activities and his subsequent denunciation of the Vietnam War resulted in his general dismissal from the art world. All his travel books, including *N by E*, *Wilderness*, *Voyaging*, *Salamina*, and *Greenland Journal*, have appeared in limited editions since his death—a tribute to their perennial appeal.

DOUG CAPRA, who currently works as a seasonal ranger for the Kenai Fjords National Park, is the author of two books on Alaska history. His articles on Rockwell Kent have appeared in such publications as *Alaska* magazine and *The Kent Collector*. He lives in Seward, Alaska, with his wife and two children. Capra wrote the introduction to the 1996 edition of *Wilderness*, also published by UPNE/WUP.